NOW YOU KNOW

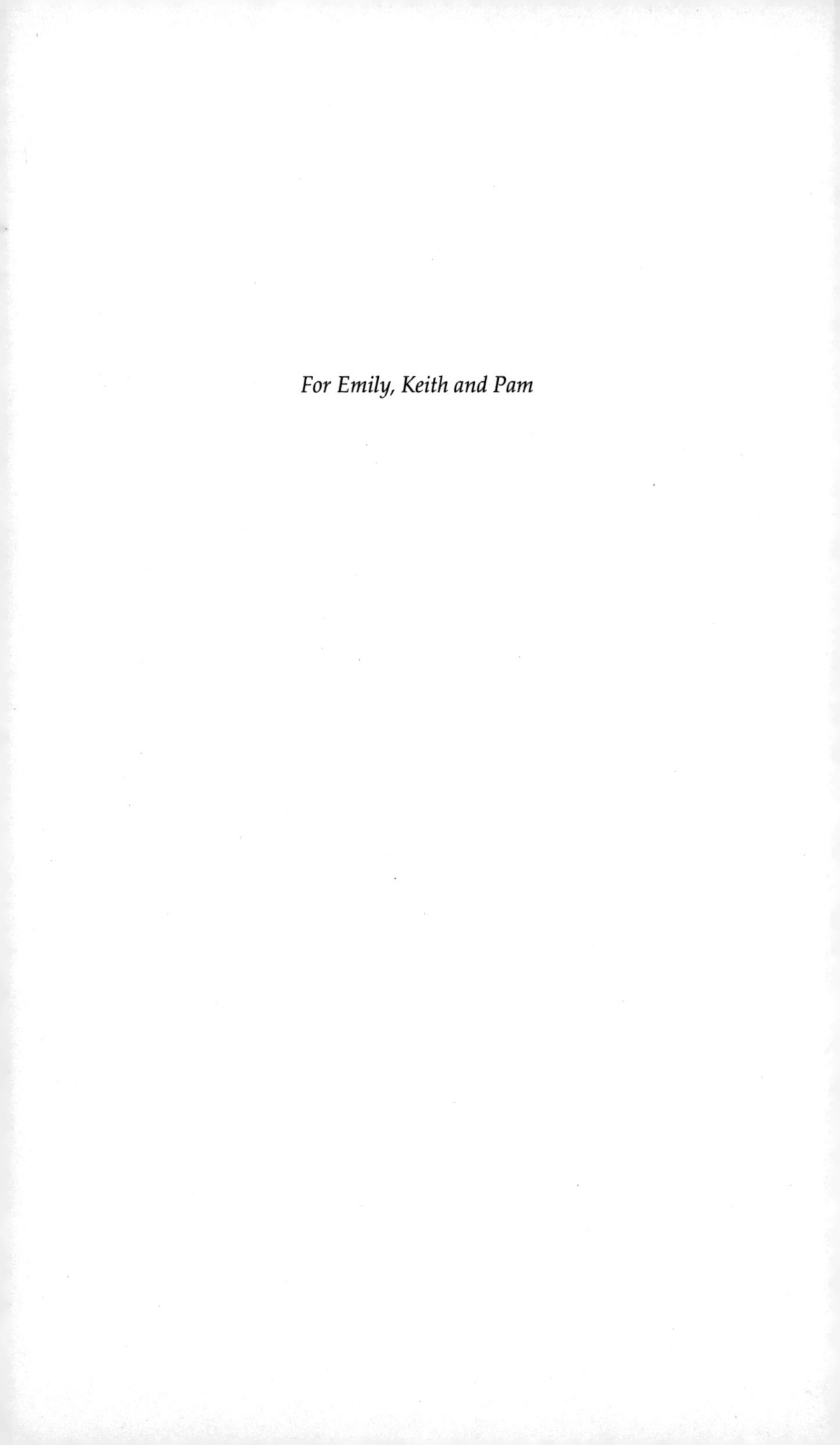

For Emily, Keith and Pam

NOW YOU KNOW

BRIAN NISBET

Brian Nisbet Publications

First published in 2015 by Brian Nisbet Publications
6 Broadwell Terrace, Dursley, GL11 4JF
www.briannisbet.com

ISBN: 978-0-9932284-0-7

Cover art © Katie Johnston
Cover photo © Hugh Beauchamp
Design © Ginny Wood

Printed, set and bound by The Printing House.

CONTENTS

FOREWORD

These high-spirited poems say it all. Nisbet's gallant collection is a festival of imagination and tenderness, generated from a mind both wide and deep in its sympathies and understanding. His dry humour, his easy facility with rhyme, his self-mockery and his craftsmanship make this poetry book a delight to discover, good not only to read but to return to and read again.

These poems come from a poet who sees his difficult life gold side up, and celebrates his world in all its brilliant facets.
Now we know indeed:

Nisbet teaches us how to treasure all we're given.

R. V. Bailey. Poet-Critic

MORNING MEDITATION

I am lying beside you, watching you
gently sleeping: the early morning sun
quietly trickles into our new life.
My head on the pillow next to yours
I can count every eyelash, like feathers
on eggshell, a soft portcullis of dreams.
The hand that held mine on a boulevard
resting semi-cupped, still speckled with paint.
Pink pyjamas, even now, forming folds
in the landscape of your elegant back.
Your rhythmic breathing, the ebb and the flow,
instills a feeling of calm, and slowly
I realise in this small attic room
I am happy.

SCHOOL CONCERT

Fat girl on the trombone
how I love you,
with your thick glasses
and puffy red legs prised into white socks.

With *molto gusto* you whack out your solo
from deep and merry farting
glissando to nimble cartwheels
and God help the right notes
if they stand in your way.

But look at that poor talented bugger
at the piano, full of promise.
With his Dad's good cufflinks,
angst set in gold,
too keenly aware
one wrong note will
infect all others,
like a malignant tumour.

But you,
you don't give a damn
about notes on a page
while there are yet
whole galaxies of sound to be heard.

Bravo!

SOCKS

I give you this simple gift of new socks
(I saw you wearing an odd pair the other day)
but please don't change, stay unorthodox
just mix up the new pairs in your own quirky way.
I'm sorry they aren't a bit more funky
but by the time I saw some with a smarter design
I'd already bought these. They may be tweedy and chunky
but, in a cold climate, sensible socks are a fine
fashion statement. I had thought
of buying the other socks as well as these
but that might overwhelm you with socks and I ought
to take it easy. But, if it would please
you, let me remove these socks in the glow
of the fire and massage you gently from heel to toe.

ON LAKE COMO

Lizards were the unexpected delight,
scampering over desiccated walls,
that pilgrimage day we climbed to St Martin's.

We rose late into the languid morning
in the Villa Belle Isole. Setting off
during the hottest part of the day
to an uphill path through an olive grove
punctuated by shrines of the rosary
for devotions of our own devising.
Tiny alert eyes observing our moves.

So we climbed in the sultry afternoon.
Reaching the top sooner than imagined
we lay down on the grass covered rocks
and devoured our picnic of white peaches,
the luscious juice dripping down our chins.

Lake Como was spread out far below us:
the paddle steamer leaving Varenna
the esplanade where we drank espresso
buses on horseshoe bends – horn obsessed,
the formal gardens of Villa Melzi.
The blueness of it all and the terracotta roofs.

NOW YOU KNOW

Wallace used to rejoice in his Lancashire heritage,
was proud to go back generations,
until he appeared on *Who Do You Think You Are*?
He then discovered the awful truth,
(we all knew but he didn't)
he was created in a workshop in Bristol,
a proper little Frankenstein.

Now he spends his days in self harm
picking lumps out of himself
and his plasticine dog.
Self knowledge is a dangerous thing.

A FEW 'HAIKU'

With the leap of Spring
the hare paints its grand opus
in the morning dew.

Dark awakening.
A conspiracy of crows
taking off en masse.

No wonder the crane,
with its knees on back to front,
walks circumspectly.

Cynical gulls mock
the flat rattle of rigging
striving to be bells.

THE ABBOT OF BINGEN

My little Abbess, I could gladly sit at your feet
to hear about the Athanasian creed or the profound
sacred note through which all the heavens resound.
But most of all let me hear about the heat
that emanates from the daughters of Eve,
which brings with it sensual delight
as with age-worn David and his Shunammite.
This is a mystery too bold to conceive,
too lively for the likes of Bernard
of Clairvaux - an eagle staring at the sun.
Or that dry old stick Pope Eugenius the Third.
Your thoughts are too verdant. Oh Hildegard,
for you all my holy orders come undone.
Let's kiss goodbye to chastity. Just say the word.

THE FARMER OF SHALLOTS

On either side the river lie
my beds of leek near four foot high.
With spuds they make a lovely pie,
enough to fully satisfy
those burghers down at Camelot.
Aliums are my delight,
my onions are a handsome sight.
I'm known to peasant, squire and Knight
as the 'Farmer of Shallots.'

It's thirty years since I was wed
and I've been faithful to our bed
but this past month what tears I've shed.
Wish I was somewhere else instead
of next to stuck-up Camelot.
We have had a pleasant life,
but one Knight's caused no end of strife
by his effect on my goodly wife,
my lady of shallots.

At forty-nine or thereabout
she'd had to let her dresses out,
she'd always been a little stout.
As for me, well I said nowt
and turned away to Camelot.

Then she vowed to stay indoors,
goodness knows what was the cause,
I've heard it called the menopause
my lady of shallots.

She said I looked just like a scruff,
my hair was wild, my hands were rough.
A farmer's life is sometimes tough.
One day she said I've had enough
my lady of shallots.
I was fairly thunderstruck
when she spurned our lovely life in muck.
She'd fallen for a fresh young buck
called bold Sir Lancelot.

Forgive me for what may be crass
my wife's no more a slip of a lass.
Where once she was an hourglass
The sand's gone south to her palliasse
thanks to cakes from Camelot.
Of course, she suits me very well,
I'm no Adonis truth to tell
and she's past being a mademoiselle
for the likes of Lancelot.

The headline in the magazine
Sir Lancelot heads to Aberdeen
she got out her knitting machine
and made him a sweater with a scene
of verdant Camelot.
It was a pretty tasteless gift
both garish and obscene
she took into the boat to drift
down-stream to Camelot.

But the time it took to dock
it had gone past twelve o'clock.
She only wore a summer frock,
the cold that night was quite a shock
in frosty Camelot.
She wore the jumper, I've been told
but the chill that night fair took a hold.
Sadly she caught her death of cold
my lady of shallots.

That is near the end of my tale,
the Knights still go in quest of the grail.
They don't care a jot for my travail.
But one Knight saw her visage pale,
good Sir Lancelot.
He said she has a lovely face
but that sweater's a pure disgrace.
That chubby woman had no taste
that lady of shallots.

MONSIEUR DEFARGE

It's our boy's birthday and my wife's not here.
She's off down the Commune, probably a mere
birthday celebration skipped her mind. She'll
be too caught up in storming the Bastille,
or tracking down the bourgeoisie. She's got
a bee in her bonnet about one lot;
it's Evremonde this and Evremonde that.
Sod them! If I was an aristocrat
I'd be on the first carriage out of here.
It hasn't always been like this - but we're
just going through a rough patch. She's no fun
anymore, always going off on one
about the suffering of the masses.
If you ask me, I blame evening classes.
Last year she did knitting and I did wood
carving, but this year from the multitude
of courses on offer she chose a dreary
option: Modern Political Theory.
She's obsessed and it is doing my head
in. We can't even snuggle up in bed
without Rousseau and bloody Robespierre,
even chopping carrots, her mind is elsewhere.
She would never miss an execution;
I've lost my wife to the Revolution.

HOME AND AWAY

I heard you playing on the radio last night, playing the Gabrieli
in the late Prom. The dog had refused to come in the house -
she started barking during your solo so I missed a bit of it, typical.
The announcer said your name at the end. I knew your solo from
you practising it while I was cooking dinner. It's funny, to hear
it coming from the Albert Hall.

I'd just got in from Sainsbury's today when you called me
from Gdansk in your break. There was a special offer on red grape
juice, so I got loads of it. So Mozart tonight: Tuesday it's Antwerp
and on Wednesday Utrecht: is that in Belgium or Holland?
Ah you don't know either, must look it up. I might go to the woods
or the canal. I could even go as far as the beach.

I'll pick you up at the station on Thursday. We'll be there,
me and the dog, to see you home.

A PERSIAN PHILOLOGY

Come my little gherkin, and be my Persian lover.
Let us feast on caviar and aubergines
on the balcony of our pagoda
to the musky strum of tambourines.

Let us feast on caviar and aubergines
in orange and lilac pyjamas
to the musky strum of tambourines
our divan strewn with roses and jasmine,

in orange and lilac pyjamas
a tapestry, a serendipity
our divan strewn with roses and jasmine
magic stars in an azure paradise

a tapestry, a serendipity
on the balcony of our pagoda
magic stars in an azure paradise.
Come my little gherkin, and be my Persian lover.

THE NAMING OF SYMPTOMS

after Henry Reed

Today we have naming of symptoms. Yesterday
we had new diagnosis and tomorrow morning
we will have what to do near the end. But today, today
we have naming of symptoms. You can have drugs:
green ones, blue ones, yellow and multi-coloured.
And today we have the naming of symptoms.

First there is Dysarthria:
That makes your speech quiet and breathy,
but not just quiet – croaky and slur the words.
You cry at inappropriate things and laugh
at the vain speech therapy exercises,
and cry at inappropriate things.

This is Bradykinesia – slowness of movement.
Your limbs freeze and you're stuck with stupid flesh
like a faulty swivel grab arm in the amusements arcade.
We have drugs for that, the only problem is
they give you Dyskinesias – involuntary movement,
but we have drugs for that.

This is Festination – small shuffling steps.
You know you have an old man's disease.
Your balance bows you forward looking to the earth,
you'll never ride your motorbike again. But
with physio you can stand on one leg,
    but you'll never ride your motorbike again.

This is Sialorrhoea – drooling and dribbling.
The trouble is in swallowing. So with a mouth full of saliva
a casual greeting goes petulantly unacknowledged.
But to drool is not cool. Botox is the thing –
add a touch of glamour to your mouth,
    but drool is definitely uncool.

This is the Consultant Neurologist.
His job is to plot your downfall;
He's marking it out in types of drugs:
'Lets just see how you get on with these.'
It's all a grand experiment. Come back in six months,
    but today we have the naming of symptoms.

IN PRAISE OF *P*

for Emma, my speech therapist

Where would we be without the letter *P*,
so perfect in its pronunciation,
excluding all phoney psychology?
Apart from relieving the population,
it promotes ping pong for perplexed people,
produces puff pastry and paella,
permits you to paint pagodas purple.
It partly puts the spin in propellers
as well as in publicists' promotions,
preserves palimpsests for posterity,
and pedals pubescent pimple potions.
Without *P* there would be no prosperity.
As put by one punter of penmanship,
'Our little life is rounded with a slee*p*.'

I BOUGHT A TRIKE ON EBAY

My neighbours think it's great fun.
Carl took time out from gardening
on a soft summer's evening
to set up the brakes and gears.

I had visions of zooming
up and down the Cotswold hills
with the dog in the basket,
grin on her face, ears flying.

It hasn't turned out that way.
It's tricky riding a trike,
and for this seeker of thrills
on wheels, three's one too many.

Ah well, I gave it a go,
but I know it's not for me.
Better to sell it on now
before the rust sets in.

THE BRAIN

It's hard to get your head around the brain.
All those ganglia, axons and neurons,
not to mention glia and myelin,
a hundred billion nerve cells
a hundred trillion interconnections:
at one per second that would take
longer than 30 million years,
extending to the spinal cord and out into the universe.

It generates its own batteries,
perception of sound, of sight,
each memory a new synapse
of the synthesis of proteins in the hippocampus.
Sense of smell in hypothalamus,
how to ride a bike, play the fiddle,
fight a war in the cerebellum
and the mysterious cortex, the seat of imagination.
Holds the secret about what makes me me and you you.
Grey matter is not so grey.
It can even rceongzie wrods taht are spleled wrnog.
All this we know.

And if we think anything at all
only the brain can tell us -
even its thoughts about itself.
Consciousness and imagination,
the perception of freewill to decide
what will I do next - there's something to think about.
To fall in love, weep, rage,
to breathe, swallow, laugh, cough
all performed without cajoling.

So when it goes wrong, you're screwed.

KINGFISHER

The kingfisher nests in an underground chamber at the end of a tunnel built by both mates. According to legend it was originally grey, but acquired its brilliant colouring when it flew near the sun while surveying the waters after the flood.

Strangely apt - that this kingfisher evokes
in all its sun emblazoned regalia
memories of Babylon, in amber
and iridescent lapis lazuli.
As if its bright winged aetiology
posits the hope of flight more luminous,
beyond destruction.

And so she brings to me a halcyon
summer. A time for casting away stones,
a time for gathering stones together
before the turning of the year.
Secluded, as in a tranquil chamber
earth rich, warm scent of moss and lavender,
a sanctuary of possibilities.
Outside the river meanders on
to somewhere else.

HOME IS WHERE THE DOG IS

Scruffy was a street dog
with a smoker's bark
tousled hair
heart of steel;
tried to conceal
how much she cared.

Sleepy head Jake
could spot a fake
at fifteen paces.
He knew mysteries,
not least, the zen
of dogginess.

Juno the turbo dog
highly sprung
propeller for a tail
burr hung ears
hose pipe tongue
a chase me grin.

My pack over years
ridiculously pleased
to greet me,
even in defeat.

A man with a dog
is never homeless.

A DASTARDLY DEED

By God, it was a dark and stormy night,
the Abbot and I were warming our feet
discussing the merits of Bakelite
a topic on which he proved most erudite
whilst outside the rain turned to sleet.

I kissed the Abbot and retired to my cell,
buckled on my equipment, tightened the strapping
to guard me from dreams that would send me to hell
(the last one with nude Eve, and Jezebel)
when I heard a quite distinct tapping.

Tap, tap, tappity tap, tap, at my window,
I'm four floors up, this must be devilish.
As I opened the latch I recited my credo
(I half expected to find Greta Garbo)
Credo in Unum De….it was a fish, a flying fish.

It flopped in, exhausted, looking close to demise,
wrung out like an exotic dishcloth.
He was lost and alone – you could tell from his eyes,
for a flying fish is a rare surprise
this far north of the Firth of Forth.

He must have been blown off course (of course)
from his greatest migratory flight.
For all noble fish must swim to their source,
but for this chap the wind must have blown with such force
he know neither birthleft nor birthright.

I offered a dram, and he didn't say no,
It was obvious he wasn't driving
for he drank like a fish, determined and slow
and the piscine comparison is so apropos
for soon he was soused as a herring.

It's a terrible thing to lose your shoal,
no wonder this fish was uptight,
but through love and compassion all is made whole
so I tucked him up in some damp kitchen roll
and bade my little guest a good night.

The next morning I fried him up in clarified butter,
a drop of Tabasco made him quite punchy.
He didn't mind, not one word did he utter,
in the end his wings gave one last little flutter
mmm, those wings were crunchy.

There is a moral to this dastardly deed
I'll tell you in just a smidgeon,
to flying fish of all species take heed
it's a tale as old as the venerable Bede
beware of organised religion.

WALKING TO PENCAITLAND

Walking out to Pencaitland with my granny
while she was still young enough,
and I was just old enough,
we discovered the overgrown pit head,
far off the beaten track.
Deserted now, except for larks
in the long summer grass.

She told me tales
of my grandfather's four mile trek
to the pit head
and as many miles underground
to the pit face.
And the anonymous young man
weeping at his funeral.
The father of my mother.
A man I only know from photographs -
in my mind confused with the Queen's father
forever embedded in an era.

Thinking of that day's walking
I stand again in that field
I reach a hand to him
as he emerges from the deep earth
into the sun.
We are about the same age,
both strangers in this landscape.

The only miners now
are old men in flat caps
coughing on the bench
at Ross's garage.

HONEYMOON IN GAIRLOCH

It was a green house, corrugated green,
a neat and decent place, washing its feet
in the peaty waters of Loch Gairloch.
Three seals impudently bobbing around,
watching out of sheer curiosity.
A place of curlews and razorbills,
each one with its various plaintive note.

This is where we begin it, you and me.
A quiet exuberance fills our days,
like our eager dog in the morning surf
or painting sea scenes for the joy of it
or tramping the hills above Sheildeig
after an indolent easy rising.
You could say we got lucky.

A KIND OF COMPASSION

With the dishcloth she wipes the tomato soup
off the jumper he has on.
No longer his past self and past caring.
After five decades of appeasement
his urge to please has finally expired,
exhausted in the minefield of butter knives,
napkin rings and the right spoon.

She has picked out his nice M&S cardigan
for the guests coming.
She resents that he comes alive then,
the old man turns on the old charm;
jovial, genial, dignified, tranquil.
Then returns again to his silent self
spent by his exertions.

She has picked out a good suit for him to wear,
the one with the subtle stripe.
He is perfectly still as she buttons his shirt.
A great weariness rests between them.
The one longs for what the other fears
in a sort of dance of duty and endurance,
a kind of compassion.

TATTIES

for Fraser Wilson

A government commission urges the drug upgrade
of a pervasive cousin of deadly nightshade.
Introduced by Walter Raleigh – it is said
alongside tobacco
its Solanum Tuberosum – be very afraid
of the deceptive potato.

Just consider the links with the drug trafficker
its origins are in South and Central America.
What do you think funded the Sandanistas
and Columbian towns?
It was Purple Congos, Edzell Blues and other exotica.
Not to mention hash browns.

Under the new Tattie Act, brackets, Scotland,
eating of spuds indoors will be banned.
Doctors will issue potato patches on demand
with slow release starch.
But Haggis, neeps and soya mash might prove so bland
protesters will march.

Golden Wonder and Cara will become passé;
only Shetland Blacks for the native gourmet.
And on special occasions, whether straight or gay
or like to cross dress,
a naughty picnic of Belle de Fontenay
or Linzer Delicatesse.

So goodbye Vanessa and Cherie and Maxine
and red skinned Desiree and Anya and Nadine
and salad days Charlotte and Nicola and Celine
I loved you all;
but especially discrete box number BF15,
we had a ball.

Please don't give in to health scaring blurb,
our variety of spuds is quite superb.
A plate without tatties is like language without verbs
(a noxious sound)
so buy yours soon from Huntly Herbs
before they go underground.

A FEW MORE 'HAIKU'

Ezra Pound's poems
good value at 50p
(don't get half of them).

The wild things sneak in.
Birdsong in a painted dome
caged divinity.

Textual intercourse.
Intimate and mischievous
like snogging with words.

Winter in April
Spring stays under her duvet
not lazy, just wise.

THE BEACH AT HUISINIS

A single track leads to Huisinis
on the western seaboard,
Land of Bailey, Malin, Hebrides.
Nowhere to go on to from here,
not a place to find explanations
in the short cropped grass.
Bleached sheep bones,
bone of my bone. Flesh of my flesh.
No lost treasure in the sand
only sand.

I am standing here
at the edge of the world.
Bewildered in dunes.

A BRIEF NOTE

I can no longer bear departures.
I am weary of loss of lovers and friends
who fade beyond the horizon
and never come back
or come back changed
or I have changed.

Yet I've done my unfair share of leaving
and never looked back, not written, not phoned,
slipped away with no explanation.
And what devastation
have I left behind?
I assumed none.

Presence is the first rule of friendship
so to all my friends; past, present and absent;
just so there is no surprise.
I am making my plans
to go into the mountains.
I have loved.

ABOUT THE AUTHOR

Brian Nisbet was born in Scotland and was then brought up and educated in Belfast during 'the troubles'. His first degree, in Semitic languages, from The Queen's University was followed by postgraduate studies in Divinity at Trinity College, Dublin. He had intended to go in to the Church but watching a production of Beckett's *Endgame* provoked a change of outlook. Instead he became a careers adviser, ultimately at the University of Sussex.

In 2007 Brian became ill with the rare and life-limiting neurological disorder, multiple systems atrophy (MSA). This movement disorder affects manual dexterity. Brian had been a keen musician but found it increasingly difficult to play any instruments so turned to writing poetry as a creative outlet unhampered by his symptoms. By then Brian was living in Aberdeenshire and had started writing with the Huntly Writers. After a move to Gloucestershire in 2010, he began studying poetry with Jenny Lewis and Jane Draycott at Oxford University.

Brian wrote the text for the BBC- commissioned work of contemporary music 'Lullaby' by Torbjörn Hultmark, broadcast on Radio 3, and has had other poems set by composers David Ward, John Kenny and Rachel Stott. His poems have been commended in the Parkinson Disease Society's Mervyn Peake Awards, and published in a number of journals. Settings of three of Brian's poems have been performed at The Edinburgh Fringe Festival. In 2013 Brian and fellow Huntly writer, Maureen Ross, were commissioned to write seven poems in response to String Quartet number 3 by Ronald Center. These were premiered at a concert in 2013, presented by James Naughtie. Brian has read his work publicly at the Oxford Fringe Literary Festival, and alongside the eminent poet R. V. Bailey in The Turning Wheel.

Brian lives in Gloucestershire with his wife the musician Emily White and their springer spaniel Juno.

ACKNOWLEDGEMENTS

are due to the editors of the following publications in which some of these poems, or versions of them, have previously appeared: **The Sentinel, Pushing Out the Boat, Poetry South, The Trombonist,** and **Spirit of the Deveron.**

I would also like to acknowledge the people who have been midwives to this publication. The editorial board: Mary Lucille Hindmarch, who has been a great facilitator and administrator, and given her time so generously; Jenny Lewis, my literary advisor and, of course, my wife Emily White 'who did the typing' and who helps me breathe.

My thanks also for practical help and encouragement to individuals: Stella Cookman, Gawain Glenton (website), Jean Hindmarch, Torbjörn Hultmark, Katie Isbester, Katie Johnston (cover art work), Morag Johnston, Wayne Reed, Maureen Ross, Jinnie Schiele, Sean Sweeney, Tessa White, Andrew White, Ginny Wood (design), and Fay Wrixon, who so successfully ran the *Kickstarter* online fund-raiser. And to the groups, Huntly Writers, and the Writers' Oxford Workshop (WOW). Nothing would have been possible without the skill and care of innumerable medical staff, especially Dr Farhad Golestani and nurse-specialist, Claire Pollock.

Generous financial support has been received through *Kickstarter* and elsewhere from: Anna Lavigne; Eric Tessier-Lavigne; Tessa & Andrew White; Geraldine Teggart & the Bristol Irish Dancing Group; Jane Walker; Jinnie Schiele; Torbjörn & Carol Hultmark; Audrey Sewell; Bill Weddle; Claire McIntyre; Edessia Rapaccioli; Gill Harris; Katie Isbester; Mick Smith; Mukta V; Nicolette Moonen & Robin Kinross; Rhonda Wheate; Sharon L; Simon de Souza; Sylvia Vetta; Thomas Brown; Walter Macdonald; Wayne A. Reed; Andy Harwood-White; Josie; Penny Bailey; Sheila McIntyre; Steve Bingham; Alix & Terry Boon; David Ward; Elinor Chambers; Gavin Poupart; Jenny Walsh; Paul Mapplebeck; Richard Benjafield; Sarah Maitland Parks; Alexander Wrixon; Joanna Merifield; Stuart James; and a number of others who have chosen to remain anonymous.